Soulful Success

Integrating Spiritual Wisdom into Your Business Journey

SHARON HESS

My website -

I dedicate this book to my son Adam and his partner Lili. They are a shining example of living mindfully in both business and life, support me in all I do, and have been a catalyst for many wonderful adventures!

Table of Contents

Preface

I created this book after many years of helping clients look at what their spiritual journey and spiritual wisdom means to them. During my work, I've uncovered time and time again how it really is about the day-to-day experiences in our life and business that matters on a spiritual path, and that there is no gap between who we are in business and personal life.

After a success business career, I owned my spiritual gifts and I have spent over the past decade using and blending the business and spiritual worlds. I believe this book talks about the spiritual side in palatable, no nonsense verbiage that is easy to incorporate no matter where you are on your spiritual journey. My first 2 books focused heavily on the spiritual nature of things, so I wanted to create one that would lean a bit more toward the business side and how this all works together. I want to acknowledge that I used AI to generate the outline and for guidance in a small amount of the content, but I assure you the majority is from my "real world" experience and understanding.

My heartfelt thanks to everyone I worked for and worked with in business, as it laid the solid foundation for understanding and succeeding in that realm. As for the Spiritual realm, I thank all of my students and all of my teachers during this incredible life journey because all of you have been both.

May you, the reader, find a nugget that leads toward your balance and harmony…

Soulful Success: Integrating Spiritual Wisdom into Your Business Journey

"Soulful Success: Integrating Spiritual Wisdom into Your Business Journey'" serves as a roadmap for readers seeking to harmonize their spiritual beliefs with their professional ambitions. This book will guide you through the transformative journey of aligning your business practices with your core values, ultimately fostering a more authentic and fulfilling approach to your business journey. By weaving spiritual wisdom into the fabric of business strategy, you will discover how to create a successful business journey that honors your soul's purpose.

The first section of the book introduces the foundational concepts of soulful success. This will explore the meaning of success from a spiritual perspective, moving beyond conventional definitions rooted in material wealth. This section emphasizes the importance of inner fulfillment and alignment with one's higher self, encouraging you to redefine success in a way that resonates with your unique spiritual journey. You will take a look at reflection exercises and thought-provoking questions, so you can begin to uncover your true motivations and understand how these insights can shape career and business endeavors.

In the following chapters, the book delves into the practical application of spiritual principles within various aspects of business. Mindfulness-based strategies will be highlighted throughout, guiding you to cultivate presence and awareness in your daily operations. Techniques such as meditation, visualization, and conscious decision- making will be introduced as tools for enhancing productivity and creativity. By integrating these practices, you will learn to navigate challenges with greater ease and clarity, fostering a work environment that is both productive and spiritually nourishing.

Next, it will also address the significance of energy healing and its impact on business professionals. You will discover how to harness the power of energy work to clear blockages, enhance intuition, and create a positive business atmosphere. This section will include practical exercises for incorporating energy healing into daily routines, helping you to maintain balance in both your personal and professional lives. By understanding the energetic dynamics at play in your business interactions, you will be empowered to create healthier, more harmonious relationships throughout your business journey.

Lastly, the book will culminate in a section dedicated to visionary business planning with a spiritual framework. This part emphasizes the importance of aligning business goals with one's soul mission and values. You will learn how to set intentions that resonate with your spiritual beliefs, creating a roadmap for success that is both purposeful and impactful. By integrating manifestation techniques and abundance mindset, the final chapters will inspire you to take bold steps toward realizing your dreams, all while remaining grounded in your spiritual truth.

Through this holistic approach, "Soulful Success" aims to equip you, the spiritual seeker, with the tools you need to thrive on your business journey while honoring your deepest self.

CHAPTER 1

The Essence of Soulful Success

Defining Soulful Success

As it is now evident, the term **Soulful Success** cannot be defined without redefining the very scope of looking at things beyond money in the bank, hierarchy in organization, etc. During the Spiritual and Energetic Journey, success is not only the physical objects or certificates possessed – it has broader aspects – realization of our own life and mission. It is possible to speak about both external and internal generic success, yet Soulful Success is when all that you are is harmoniously integrated with what you do to further the aspirations of professional success. Soulful Success is always oriented on being fulfilled spiritually as well. In its most blended essence, all success is related to the consideration of psychological aspects and in this case, it is spiritual achievement with the inner aspect of success orientation.

Embedded within the concept of Soulful Success is the understanding of the necessity to know yourself fully and the goals that you are trying to achieve. It has been demonstrated that a mindful approach helps in knowing the specific factors that a person's intentions are based on, so that what is intended will be acted upon. This insight helps in differentiating what society is expecting from you and what you want to do, thus you follow <u>your</u> path. Mindfulness practices such as meditation and reflective writing are tools for this journey that create clarity and understanding that helps in decision-making, especially in the personal and work realms.

Additionally, the concept of Soulful Success is about giving and making a difference. In a highly individualistic society, you can find those who are in their soulful states that believe that your success lies in taking care of other people as well as yourself. This way of thinking leads to a transformation from a cut-throat competition view to team and community building. For business-minded spiritual people, success entails starting organizations that grow not just in net worth but also in the ability to touch and lift other peoples' lives. Such a method makes sure that the tasks undertaken carry a weight of meaning as well as the outcome being more than a preoccupation with oneself.

One of the characteristics of Soulful Success is uniting spiritual and business thinking. For example, spiritual life and business coaching helps individuals understand how to structure their businesses and the practices of the business in alignment with their spirituality. This measurement of success could be imbedded in such practices as having a sense of ethical responsibility with one's business and nurturing of positive workplace culture rather than only looking at profit. Businesses controlled by spiritual values give those entrepreneurs the strength to bear each obstacle that dares get in their way and helps them build economically successful businesses that realize their purposes.

In the end, defining Soulful Success is about purposely leading a life full of happiness. Understand and know that each of you is on the right path as success is not a place but a constant journey in seeking it. With the right approach toward obtaining work-life balance, vision-making, and manifestation you will also create a business environment that is in keeping with your spirituality. For many, embracing Soulful Success means that business or work can be a means of healing self and society for the good of the Universe.

The Intersection of Spirituality and Business

In this time of new enterprise ideas, something in the line of "spirit business" has evolved, which integrates spirituality into business. This integration empowers both spiritual practitioners and business specialists to achieve their inner archetypes and integrate them into their professional lives for overall well-being. Spirituality, which can be described as the intrinsic need of individuals to seek meaning in life, is an adjunct to the entrepreneur as it nurtures the individual's originality, sense of purpose, and optimism. Striving for business goals while also staying true to yourself can be achieved by incorporating spiritual teachings into your business.

Employing a mindful approach within businesses can be a very good common ground for this because it makes clear that a certain desired state must be achieved in every aspect of business including the lesser-known ones. It is helpful because this aspect of mindfulness helps in gaining clarity to decide not only the tactical actions of businesses but the ethical considerations as well. This encourages both managers and entrepreneurs to create conditions where creativity and innovation are encouraged leading to sustainable businesses whose focus is not on profits only. The ability to cope with difficulties and keep inner peace, which is so necessary for business, can be improved by applying mindfulness to day-to-day activities.

Soulful success takes this combination one notch higher by anchoring you in understanding your special talents and how those talents can serve the world. This encourages you to look for the reason behind doing things, which then strengthens a deeper connection to your vision and purpose. Consequently, the business offerings are more meaningful for your clients because they are designed to meet the customers' genuine needs because the business goals are interwoven in a spiritual context. This integration bolsters the well-being of the individual and also invites ideal clients into the fold of a community built on shared values and support.

Alternately, energy healing can also prove to be pivotal here. For business people, understanding and harnessing energy dynamics can lead to a more harmonious work environment and improved interpersonal relationships. Techniques like Reiki and chakra balancing are two such methods that can be rather handy when trying to develop one's intuition, creativity and emotional intelligence. When you address energetic blockages, you release negativity and bring in a sense of balance. A positive energy flow will help you find resilience and clarity so that you can withstand stressful situations and to see logic in ambiguity.

Last but not least, Soulful Success stresses that your business journey also calls to the spiritual part in you. This approach encourages you to seek careers or business opportunities that are not only financially rewarding but also fulfilling on a soul level. By integrating spiritual practices into business and career planning, you can manifest abundance while maintaining a work-life balance that honors your spiritual journey. Through this visionary approach that incorporates spiritual frameworks, you can chart a course that reflects your deepest values, ultimately leading to soulful success that enriches both your life and the lives of those they serve.

Why Spiritual Seekers Need a Different Approach

When seeking to develop themselves, spiritual seekers often find themselves on a very different terrain that does not conform to the norms of the business world. It is often common to find that the pursuit of a spiritual journey is highly dependent on self-awareness, considering the consciousness of the universe, and the desire to align work with value. This unique perspective requires a different approach to business, one that honors intuition, mindfulness, and holistic well-being. This business view can be developed with ease but there is a reversal of mind and theories of conduct. The business-as-usual approach which surrounds itself with the practices of strategies geared toward the bottom-line profit, especially with cut-throat competition, may not suit those whose work is seen as part of a spiritual journey.

This could present a big problem when most of your goals require you to think differently. Generally, business professionals may be satisfied with a profit-based definition of success. People on a spiritual journey are more focused on advancement with purpose, impact, and value congruency. This change in thought comes with the requirement of a new business model that welcomes spirituality allowing you to find a sense of joy and fulfillment in your work. When you incorporate strategies that emphasize self-awareness and mindfulness you can create a business or follow a career path where you can thrive financially while also contributing positively to the world.

Furthermore, the energy factor is very important in the lives of those interested in spiritual practices. In the field of energy medicine as well as all intuitive practices, the performance of a business can depend greatly upon the knowledge and control of the energy. To this understanding, it becomes evident that some other additional tools and techniques must be used that are beyond the conventional only. Routine activities such as meditation, visualization, and energy clearing can help to unleash the creative mind, make sound choices, and withstand pressures better.

When you think about energy remember this is a vibrational Universe. Tiny vibrating strings of energy make up every particle in the Universe, according to Sera Cremonini and other string theorists. The theory also allows the possibility of additional dimensions beyond space and time. You and everything around you has a specific vibration, or energetic make-up, and many things contribute to your energy and how your energy changes and flows. The important thing to remember is that through realizing and managing your innate energy you will be able to create a fertile ground for new developments and a more abundant and meaningful business journey.

Yet another important area to pay attention to is work-life balance, particularly for spiritual seekers. Most spiritual persons have a strong focus on wellness and personal development and seek to integrate work and life purpose whenever possible. To do this, they need ways of creating harmony and balance between their personal and professional lives. Strategies like mindfulness-based business strategies or the assistance of a spiritual business coach will help you set healthy boundaries, prioritize your time for self-care, and infuse spiritual practices into everyday life. Not only do balanced pursuits result in increased productivity, but also in growing emotionally and spiritually.

Business planning should aim to include a visionary element... spiritual framework that allows you to dream big and connect with your values. Incorporating your values on your business journey will help you actually visualize what your ideal outcomes could look like, manifest your goals through intention, and take focused action toward those ideals. In that way, you'll find clarity and confidence as you work your way through the sometime overwhelming complexities of business.

What makes this integration of the journey so enriching is that it inspires not only oneself, but others, too, creating ripples that one day may very well revolutionize the business landscape into a more conscious, more compassionate model aligned with the greater good. You are being called to take on a different way-one that honors your own inside-out wisdom and opens doors to Soulful Success not only for you but for others too.

CHAPTER 2

Spiritual Foundations for Business

Understanding Your Core Values

Understanding your core values is one of the prime ingredients in creating and sustaining a soulful, successful business. Your core values will be guideposts that help form your decisions, actions, and interactions both personally and professionally. As you weave core values into your business practices, you'll be able to tap deeper into your purpose and authenticity. This will not only attract clients who resonate with your mission but also foster a harmonious work environment-a reflection of your spiritual beliefs.

This integration is of great value not only for your own development but also for motivating others and creating a transforming effect that encourages the business world to be more aware and considerate, working in the right direction. Quite frankly, as you walk your spiritual path, you are challenged to take a different business journey, one that respects your gut feelings and the pursuit of genuine fulfillment for yourself as well as those around you.

The first step in taking this journey is understanding what really matters to you. What are your core values? Most often, the birth of core values comes through your experiences, your belief system, and how you have grown from life experiences. Think about those times when your life was changed in gigantic ways. What themes or principles came forward regarding those life-changing experiences?

Take some time to reflect on the characteristics of others that inspire you, and then envision which of these characteristics you may have a personal urge to share with others. In this way you can start to identify what main values will form the basis of your business and spiritual practices. Journaling about your ideas or sharing them with your spiritual mentor or coach will give you a much better idea of what matters most to you deep down.

Once you have figured out what is important to you, the next line of action is how these values can be incorporated into the business model. This can be in the form of the way you communicate to the clients and the way projects are handled as well as other purposes. For example, if 'compassion' is one of your core values, focus on what the client needs most so that you can help them more authentically. It not only boosts your credibility but also, makes a positive difference in the lives of the people you assist. By consciously embedding your values into your business operations, you cultivate an environment where your spiritual and professional aspirations can thrive together.

It is also important that you go back and revisit your core values regularly. As life happens, as you are developing and new realizations become foremost in your understanding, things that seemed to matter shift, and what is truly important to you is called into question. Allow this process to naturally happen within you. Take time out to review and reflect if your core values are still relevant and are you finding ways to express them in business?

This becomes a constantly ongoing process where you are always double-checking that your business is truly a reflection of who you are at any one time. Because, as you change and grow through your spiritual pathway, your offerings will, by nature, start to shift to accommodate that. Your main purpose may not necessarily be different, but the way in which you offer it to the world does change.

Finally, if you understand your core values, it might raise your ability to manifest abundance and work-life balance spectacularly. When your business practices happen in conjunction with values that resonate with your soul, you make a more satisfying and sustained business journey. The authenticity of your mission will attract clients and collaborators alike creating the possibility of growth and success.

Nurture a space that reflects and respects your core values, and in return, you nurture not only yourself but also the universal consciousness toward a kinder and more connected commercial ecosystem.

EXERCISE –

Identifying your core values can be a very potent way to achieve self-awareness and guide decisions. Here's an engaging exercise you can use:

Step 1: Reflect on Meaningful Experiences

Instructions: Reflect back on your life, considering three to five experiences when you have felt most fulfilled, proud, or in touch with a higher sense of purpose. These may be achievements, relationships, moments of service, or overcoming challenges.

Journal Prompt:

- What happened during each experience?
- What were you proud of
- What felt fulfilling
- What inspired you?
- Who were you with and did that affect the experience?

Step 2: Identify Values in Those Experiences

Instructions:

Take each of those experiences that you have listed and write down what values underlie them.

EXAMPLES –

If one experience was called helping a friend in need, the value could be "compassion" or "service."

If it was accomplishing something you personally had a hard time doing-a difficult personal goal-the value could be "determination" or "growth."

Journal Prompt:

- What values were being honored during these experiences?
- Which personal qualities or ways of behaving were most crucial in making those moments special?

EXAMPLES:

Experience - Volunteering in a shelter. Value is in service, compassion and kindness

Experience - Having run a marathon. Values are tenacity, self-discipline, health

<u>Step 3: Consider a Set of Core Values</u>

Instructions:

Below is a list of common core values. Review this list and circle or highlight any that resonate with you. Feel free to add your own as well.

Sample Values List:

- Integrity
- Creativity
- Adventure
- Honesty
- Respect
- Freedom
- Responsibility
- Spirituality
- Learning
- Love
- Courage
- Empathy
- family
- Success
- Gratitude
- Happiness

- Service
- Health
- Balance
- Security
- Confidence

Step 4-Narrow Down Your Core Values

Instructions: Once you have a list of several values, reduce to your Top 5 Core Values. This is a list of the values with which you most closely identify and through which most important decisions would be considered.

Reflection Prompt:

Which values feel most important to who you are?

Which one of these values is more meaningful to you than the rest?

My Top 5 Core Values:

1. ___________________
2. ___________________
3. ___________________
4. ___________________
5. ___________________

Step 5: Apply Your Values to Real-Life Scenarios

Instructions: Think about a current situation or decision you're facing. Write it down and consider how your core values can help guide your choice or action.

EXAMPLE:

Decision: Whether to take another job OR a different type of client Reflection - Will this job (new type of client) provide me with those very crucial things: creativity, freedom, and growth?

Journal Prompt:

How does this relate to your core values?

How would living your values in this case feel compared to not living them?

Step 6: Reflection on Core Values at Work in Everyday Life

Instructions: Take a moment to reflect, after this exercise is complete, on how your core values impact your everyday actions. Set an intention to consciously live in alignment with your values.

Journal Prompt: -

In what ways do you already honor your values in daily life?

Which changes can you do to make you more in alignment with your core values?

This exercise lets you take a closer look at not only your core values but also how those values come into play in real-life situations becoming a bridge between self-awareness and actionable living.

Aligning Your Business with Your Spiritual Path

Bringing your business or career into alignment with your spiritual path is quite a journey that requires soul searching and intentionality. For Soulful Success to be found, alignment needs to take place, wherein you have to create a business, or be aligned with a business, that really resonates with your core values and higher purpose. In fact, when your business life is an extension of your spirituality, it is filled with purpose and takes on a whole new dimension of passion as you draw to yourself clients and opportunities that resonate with your true nature. This subchapter highlights the integration of one's spiritual journey into your business journey.

Let's start this alignment process by first engaging in deep self-exploration to ascertain what spirituality means to you. Think about how you define success and how your beliefs values or even experiences have contributed to shaping your vision of success.

EXERCISE –

DISCOVERING WHAT SPIRITUALITY MEANS TO YOU

EXERCISE Discovering what spirituality means to you is a personal journey that requires self-reflection, exploration, and an openness to new ideas and experiences.

1. <u>Self-Reflection: Start with What You Know</u>

• Ask Questions:

What does spirituality mean to you at this moment.?
Do you link it to religion, a feeling of connection, inner peace, or something else entirely?

Example Prompts to Reflect On:

- What does the idea of a "higher power" or greater force mean to me?
- When do I feel most connected to myself, others, or the world around me?
- How do I define concepts like peace, love, and purpose?
- How does spirituality fit into my everyday life? Does it need to?
- What does my intuition tell me about the meaning of life and my place in it?

• Explore Feelings:

Think about times when you've experienced peace, awe, or a connection to something larger than yourself. These moments can reveal what spirituality signifies for you.

• Journaling: Write down your beliefs, values, and experiences that have led you to question or affirm a deeper meaning in life.

2. <u>Explore Different Paths</u>

- Read and Research: Find books, spiritual teachers, podcasts etc. from various spiritual traditions such as Buddhism, Sufism, mysticism, or philosophy. Diving into diverse ideas can help clarify your own beliefs.
- Attend Events: Consider going to workshops, gatherings, meditation classes, religious services etc. to understand others point of view to help clarity your own.
- Talk to People: Engage in conversations with individuals who hold different views on spirituality. This can help you identify what resonates with you and what doesn't.

3. <u>Engage in Different Practices</u>

- Meditation or Prayer: There are different forms of meditation you can look into or use of prayer can lead to a deeper understanding of your inner self.
- Nature: Spend time outdoors, as it often inspires a sense of wonder and connection. Pay attention to your feelings during these experiences.
- Creative Expression: Engage in art, music, or writing as spiritual practices. Use these creative outlets to explore and express your inner thoughts and emotions.

4. <u>Notice What Resonates</u>

- Listen to Your Intuition: Notice what feels true and authentic to you. Spirituality is a very personal thing and isn't about adopting someone else's beliefs but discovering what resonates with your inner being.
- Follow Your Curiosity: When you feel drawn to something or it interests you, explore it more deeply. Your curiosity can be a guidance to what holds spiritual significance for you.

5. <u>Be Open to Change</u>

- Allow Evolution: Your understanding of spirituality will likely change over time. Be open to evolving your beliefs as you learn and grow.

- Release Expectations: Don't pressure yourself to arrive at a definitive answer. The journey itself is spiritual, and it's okay if your definition shifts along the way.

6. Integrate and Live It

- Apply It to Your Life: Once you begin to get a sense of what spirituality means to you, start to integrate it into your daily life. Whether through kindness, gratitude, or mindful living, bring your spirituality into your actions.
- Reflect Often: Keep coming back to the question of what spirituality means to you. As you move through different stages of life, your understanding may deepen or shift.

This process isn't about finding "the right" answer, but discovering what feels true to you. Each person's spiritual path is unique, and allowing yourself to explore without judgment can lead to a richer, more fulfilling understanding of spirituality.

———

Other things to consider when aligning your business with your spiritual path is looking into meditation, journaling, energy-healing and other spiritual practices that help you clarify your intentions and goals which we will look into more later.

If you find yourself stuck or when you do not know where to look, a spiritual coach or other practitioners can assist you in connecting the dots. It is of vital importance to ground your business life in your spiritual understanding so you build your business life with a strong foundation to guide your decisions and actions. This clarity is important because it empowers you to support other people on their journeys and remain true to your own.

Mindfulness can also be a potent tool to help you align your business with your spiritual path. Use of mindfulness-based strategies in everyday operations will help you develop better focus, be more creative, and become emotionally resilient. You will be enabled to be aware of what you are thinking, feeling, or doing, and thereby make conscious choices about things which can reflect your spiritual values. This approach takes into consideration personal well-being, professional growth, and thus allows for balance in energy as well as work-life balance. When mindfulness is emphasized, it become easier to be present; it reduces stress and allows serving your clients in a very genuine way.

Always think about visionary business planning with a spiritual framework. Planning businesses with a spiritual context in mind will actually help further entwine these two concepts of your spirituality and business goals. More often than not, this means setting an intention based not merely on monetary return but on the good one wishes to bring into the world. Building a business model that incorporates spiritual principles will ideally fit within an organizational framework that supports your mission and calls to your higher purpose.

Your journey will be opened to seeing more of your dreams through the use of vision boards, manifestation techniques, and goal setting, then taking the steps to make them real, which I will address in more depth in another chapter. Use of these things may even bring a change to how you look to integrate the business with your spiritual path. A lot of people who are spiritually searching often hold negative connotations of money and/or people who are successful, which according to them does not conform to spirituality. However, these groups of people need to change their mindsets and understand and even embrace the idea that it is fine to be wealthy. There is nothing spiritual about living in lack!

Embracing a mindset of abundance is crucial to aligning your business with your spiritual journey. Most spiritual seekers limit their beliefs in money and success, believing these are oxymorons to any spiritual path. Reframe your thinking to understand that abundance is a natural state of being...and it will attract into your life and business. This shift in consciousness will not only help in personal growth but also empower you to lead others in their manifestation journeys.

Eventually, what happens is that the alignment of a business with your spiritual path creates a gratifying and sustainable practice that respects your purpose and serves both your needs and those of the greater community.

The Role of Intuition in Decision-Making

When striving for Soulful Success there is one thing that easily stands out as a must, which is intuition when it comes to decision-making because using your intuition helps in clarifying the many options available. For you as a spiritual seeker, bringing intuition into the decision-making process is not merely an abstract concept; it is a practical tool that can help you look deeper into how to achieve authentic success. Intuition – commonly referred to as a 'gut feeling' or 'knowing' – is a concept that functions between the activity of the conscious brain and deeper levels of consciousness where non-logic-based knowledge lies, which can lead to ideas that are otherwise hard to conceive simply by analysis.

Recognizing intuition's foundation in mindfulness and presence is the first step toward comprehending its function in our decision-making. We create the space for visceral understandings to emerge once we work to increase our awareness of our thoughts and emotions. Mindfulness practice encourages us to pay attention to both our inner voice and our logical thoughts, which are frequently crucial to determining our true goals and desires. By continuously improving our ability to pay attention to our thoughts and emotions, we align ourselves with the flow of universal energy, which enables us to tap into intuitive guidance. In doing so, we can steer our business journey toward greater alignment with our soul's purpose.

Intuition plays a special role in business for soul-centered entrepreneurs when it's time to make a strategic decision about a new product launch, business model change, or partnership. When seeking clarity and confidence, intuition can come to the rescue! Soul-centered professionals leverage any known information with thinking "outside the box" and this way of looking at things creates a holistic way rather than a pure number-crunching exercise. Such a process enables you to choose in a manner that encompasses all the alternatives providing the deepest satisfaction as well as aligning with the central strategic objective.

Apart from mindfulness, the practice of energy healing can also be a great weapon in improving one's ability to be intuitive. As a result of releasing any energy blocks or restrictions and encouraging energy flow, people can develop vast awareness and attention to inner guidance. This process can be enhanced through practices such as meditation, visualization, and even energy healing from a practitioner to help you connect with your guidance. It gets easier to make decisions that resonate with your inner voice, which will, in turn, give satisfying results to the mind, body, and soul.

Finally, it is trust and practice that enables one to build a healthy relationship with their intuition. As it is with any other skill set that takes time to apply with adequate help, so can the ability to separate intuition from fear and doubt. Keeping a log of such instances, practicing introspection from time to time, and consulting a spiritual business coach would further assist in this venture. While developing intuition as a part of the decision-making process, you not only improve your business skills but also get one step closer to your ideal life. It is in this manner that Intuition stops being only a function of decision-making but rather, a transcended element of engaged success.

CHAPTER 3

Mindfulness-Based Business Strategies

The Power of Mindfulness in the Workplace

In today's business world where things move quickly and change rapidly for those looking to blend their beliefs with their work life; the idea of mindfulness is gaining traction as a valuable tool, for both personal business growth. Mindfulness involves being fully present in each moment and cultivating a sense of awareness that can positively impact how we interact in our work environment. Practicing mindfulness doesn't just benefit individuals by boosting their well-being; it also enhances team productivity and innovation when incorporated into both routines and relationships at work. By making mindfulness a part of interactions and habits while working, professionals can strike a balance between satisfaction and business.

The ability of mindfulness to help people develop their emotional intelligence in the workplace is one of it's main advantages. Business mentors emphasize how crucial emotional intelligence and regulation are to team dynamics and leadership. By encouraging self-awareness in the workplace through mindfulness exercises, people are better equipped to react to challenges thoughtfully rather than with "knee jerk" responses. This thoughtful approach to emotion regulation fosters an environment at work where everyone feels valued. By integrating mindfulness into their daily routines, leaders can significantly enhance their relationships and develop their skills, which is essential for establishing a productive workplace.

Putting mindfulness-based business strategies into practice can also lead to better attention and clear thinking, which are crucial for success in both personal and professional contexts. You can clear your thoughts and increase your ability to maintain concentration on your everyday tasks by engaging in mindfulness practices like meditation or conscious breathing exercises. In addition to increasing productivity, this mental clarity fosters innovation and efficient troubleshooting techniques. Mindfulness is essential for those who are committed to creating a business endeavor that is focused on their vision and ideals in the face of distractions because it helps them to remain aligned with their core beliefs and long-term objectives.,

Furthermore, being mindful is a critical key in maintaining a balance between work and personal life, something many people value as a part of their journey. Making mindfulness a part of your routine will help you remember to focus on self-care and establish boundaries that promote well-being avoiding exhaustion. This helps create a nurturing and self-aware approach to work. By pausing at points during the day you can realign with your goals and reenergize yourself resulting in a more satisfying and efficient work environment. Maintaining this equilibrium is important not just for your welfare, but also for the overall health of any business.

Mindfulness in the workplace goes beyond personal advantages as it can lead to a positive culture change in organizations when adopted widely by businesses. It fosters environments that value empathy, collaboration and purpose. These shifts are particularly meaningful for individuals on a spiritual path as they emphasize that success is not about money but about making a positive difference, in people's lives and the world.

Incorporating mindfulness into your business strategies will help you create a more purposeful journey as you align daily decisions with your spiritual goals and core values. When you do, you will manifest a more abundant and meaningful business with greater ease.

Techniques for Cultivating Mindfulness

For those on a spiritual path who are also dealing with the difficulties and complexities of the business world, mindfulness practice becomes essential. Being self-aware is only one aspect; another is connecting with your objectives and driving forces. You can create a foundation for meaningful success by implementing mindfulness practices into your daily routine. These strategies improve your ability to manage stress, concentrate, and make decisions that align with your values, which leads to a more well-rounded business strategy.

One way to cultivate mindfulness into your daily routine is to meditate. You can set aside time each day for meditation as well as other self-calming activities that help you connect with yourself. Meditation can be approached in a variety of ways, such as by concentrating on your breathing or using guided imagery. You can improve your awareness and mental clarity by meditating for a short while each day. In addition to preparing the mind for solutions, this mindful state helps maintain composure in the midst of the hectic business world.

Intentional observation is another effective strategy. This method fosters a deeper appreciation for the present by encouraging people to fully interact with their surroundings and experiences. Whether in a brainstorming session, meeting, or just taking a stroll in the outdoors, spending some time observing thoughts, feelings, and sensations without passing judgment can greatly improve one's capacity to remain grounded. You can learn to react to situations thoughtfully rather than impulsively by engaging in mindful observation, which will help you make more deliberate and purposeful decisions.

Incorporating breathwork into daily routines is another valuable mindfulness technique. Breath serves as a bridge between the mind and body, and conscious breathing can help alleviate feelings of stress and anxiety that often accompany the business journey. Practicing deep, intentional breaths—especially during moments of tension—can bring an immediate sense of calm and clarity, allowing you to reconnect with your purpose and vision. Regular breathwork can also enhance creativity and focus, providing a fresh perspective on challenges and opportunities.

Lastly, journaling as a mindfulness practice can be transformative for you in business. Keeping a journal allows for reflection and self-discovery, enabling you to articulate your thoughts, feelings, and aspirations. By writing regularly, you can track progress, identify patterns, and clarify goals, all of which contribute to a deeper understanding of your spiritual path. This practice not only fosters self-awareness but also serves as a tool for manifestation, as you can articulate your intentions and visualize your goals in alignment with your highest values. Through these techniques, you can cultivate a mindful approach to business endeavors, leading to Soulful Success that resonates with your true self.

Implementing Mindfulness in Business Practices

A transformative strategy that harmonizes professional pursuits with spiritual values is the application of mindfulness in business practices. A more peaceful workplace, better decision-making, and stronger bonds with clients and/or team members can all result from incorporating mindfulness into daily operations. At its essence, mindfulness teaches present moment awareness that when raised to a higher quality — clarity and focus rooted in the sensory world not just thought or emotion but deep within sensation of the physical realm — is essential for anyone struggling with navigating modern business. In order to promote a more soulful approach to success, this section will examine doable tactics for integrating mindfulness into different facets of daily operations.

To begin with, mindfulness can be seamlessly woven into the fabric of organizational culture. This starts with leadership (which is you if you are a solopreneur) embodying mindfulness principles, which sets the tone for the business. You can initiate daily mindfulness practices such as meditation or brief moments of silence before meetings to center yourself or if a leader, your team. By establishing an environment that prioritizes presence and awareness, businesses can enhance emotional intelligence and empathy among all individuals involved with the business. This not only improves interpersonal relationships but also creates a supportive atmosphere where creativity and collaboration can flourish.

Incorporating mindfulness into decision-making processes is another critical aspect of its implementation. In most cases, business decisions are made under pressure in response to certain conditions and with the view of achieving certain outcomes within a given span of time. Using mindfulness techniques like reflective pauses you are able to take a step back and look at things in a more analytical way. This approach helps gives more weight to overall impact since you can now examine how the decision will affect the organizational impact and its stakeholder by remembering to guide the decision by the organization's vision and values. Additionally, this practice helps you avoid making snap decisions and makes it possible for you to manifest outcomes in line with your ethical and spiritual beliefs.

In addition, mindfulness promotes positive customer interactions and relations. Mindfulness helps you be more attentive to clients and customers, to listen to what they are saying and to respond in kind. This creates a more profound level of trust and rapport – prerequisites for any sort of enterprise. Using active listening and empathy, you can get to the bottom of what your clients really need so you can implement proper solutions. This alignment with the client values and their goals makes them loyal and also creates a pool of like-minded people who embrace the concept of Soulful Success.

Finally, the use of mindfulness techniques in work-life balance is crucial for avoiding burnout and keeping work and spiritual pursuit balanced. Spiritual seekers are faced with a dilemma of balancing work and ambition with self-care for their souls. Mindfulness is a way to make you stay motivated and focused on your mental, emotional and spiritual well-being as well as your business. It is important to take mindful breaks, keep a gratitude journal, and reflect regularly to help you remember why you are doing what you are doing and bring your business-related activities back to their purpose. With a balanced approach and attitude, you will be able to approach both your work and life purpose and harmoniously achieve the goal of Soulful Success in all spheres of life.

MINDFUL EXERCISES

MINDFUL BREATHING –

Take a comfortable seat and concentrate on your breathing.

Breath in to the count of four, hold it for four counts, and then release it for four counts.

Do this for three to five minutes.

Journal Prompt:

Write about how your mood changed as a result of concentrating on your breathing after the exercise.

- Were you distracted by anything in your mind?
- In what way did you return to the present?

MINDFUL LISTENING

Spend five to ten minutes sitting in a quiet place and listening to music or the sounds around you. Make an effort to observe each detail objectively and without bias. Pay attention to how each instrument, voice, or background noise sounds.

Journal Prompt:

- What aspects of the music or sound caught your attention that you had not previously noticed?
- What impact did listening intently have on your sense of presence?

MINDFUL OF YOUR FIVE SENSES

Sit comfortably and take a few deep breaths. Now, go through each of your five senses, identifying:

- 5 things you can see
- 4 things you can touch
- 3 things you can hear
- 2 things you can smell
- 1 thing you can taste

Journal Prompt:

- How did this exercise shift your awareness?
- Did it change how you were feeling emotionally or physically?
- How long did it take to become fully immersed in the present?

CHAPTER 4

Soul-Centered Entrepreneurship

What it Means to Be a Soul-Centered Entrepreneur

The idea of being a Soul-Centered Entrepreneur embraces the very idea of Soulful Success, offering a transformative approach to business. This paradigm moves the emphasis away from purely profit-driven goals and toward a comprehensive viewpoint that combines spiritual development, genuine connection, and personal growth. Being a soul-centered entrepreneur entails matching your business practices with your highest values, purpose, and vision because you are passionate about incorporating your core beliefs into your professional endeavors. It is about accepting the path of entrepreneurship as a profound practice of self-discovery and service to others, rather than merely as a way to achieve a monetary goal.

Realizing that every business encounter is a chance to bring your spiritual ideals to life is the foundation of soul-centered entrepreneurship. This entails developing genuine relationships, making decisions with mindfulness, and establishing an environment at work that embodies integrity and compassion. Soul-Centered Entrepreneurs place a high value on ethical behavior, community involvement, and thoughtful communication because they know that their influence goes beyond any business dealings. It's about improving your own well-being and making a positive impact on your clients' and the community's lives by incorporating spiritual principles into your day-to-day operations.

The dedication to spiritual and personal growth is one of the Soul-Centered Entrepreneur's main themes. Along the way, this path necessitates constant self-reflection and observation, as well as the ability to handle challenges as a learning opportunity. In addition to improving an entrepreneur's health, spiritual practices like visualization, energy healing, and meditation aid in the manifestation of abundance. There will therefore be no obstacles in the way of realizing your business aspirations if, as a soul-centered entrepreneur, you are able to match your objectives with your spiritual principles.

Moreover, soul-centered entrepreneurship emphasizes the importance of work-life balance through spiritual practices. By integrating rituals and mindfulness techniques into your daily routines, you can cultivate a sense of harmony between your professional and personal life. This balance is essential for maintaining energy levels, fostering creativity, and preventing burnout. Entrepreneurs who prioritize their spiritual well-being inspire others around them to do the same, creating a ripple effect that promotes a healthier, more balanced approach to work and life.

Finally, being a soul-centered entrepreneur is all about creating something that is firmly grounded in authenticity and purpose; a vision of the soul. This approach demands the willingness to link one's business objectives with a larger purpose that benefits both the self and others. For those who are on the spiritual journey, this approach makes them financially wealthy while at the same time giving them fulfillment and happiness, which is what Soulful Success is all about. Through the infusion of spirituality into business experience, soul-centered entrepreneurs establish a legacy beyond the conventional business model and make a positive and lasting impression on your clients, communities and the world in general.

Identifying Your Unique Gifts and Talents

Identifying your unique gifts and talents is a transformative journey that serves as the foundation for aligning your business endeavors with your authentic self. As a spiritual seeker, you possess an inherent wisdom that can guide you toward recognizing the innate abilities that set you apart. These gifts may include intuitive insights, creative expression, or the ability to connect deeply with others. By exploring and acknowledging these talents, you can begin to craft a business that resonates with both your personal values and your professional aspirations.

To start this exploration, consider engaging in mindful practices such as meditation or any of the previous mindfulness exercises to first tune into your inner voice and quiet the noise of external influences. Once you do, try these exercises...

EXERCISE #1

Think back to your childhood and remember activities that made you feel alive, excited, and lost in time. Often, the things we were drawn to as children reflect our innate talents.

Journal Prompt

- What did I enjoy as a child that made me lose track of time?
- Write down at least five activities or hobbies from your childhood and reflect on how they connect in your current life.

EXERCISE #2

Reflect on moments when as an adult you felt particularly fulfilled or energized.

Journal Prompt:

- What activities made you lose track of time?
- What feedback have you received from peers, mentors, or clients that highlights your strengths?

Journaling about these reflections can illuminate patterns and themes that point to your unique gifts, making it easier to integrate them into your business approach.

Another effective way to identify your talents is through the lens of energy healing.

Each person has a unique energetic signature that vibrates at a specific frequency. By engaging in energy work, such as Reiki, chakra balancing, looking into your soul story and soul make up, etc., you can enhance understanding some of your readily available energetic gifts. There are many practitioners that focus on helping you with this if you find yourself stuck. Ask others what modality or practice did they find most helpful.

Confronting any limiting beliefs that may have prevented you from reaching your full potential can go a long way in discovering your gifts. This requires you to challenge any limitations that you placed on yourself in the past for unfounded reasons. For many on a spiritual journey, issues such as the impostor syndrome or fear of being judged causes one to lose sight of their worth. We will look at limiting beliefs more later but when they come up, try to accept these emotions without any criticism and think about changing the story you tell yourself. This is where a spiritual coach can be particularly helpful because they can look at what you are unable to see and come up with strategies on how to change your belief system.

Also, workshops, online support or local gatherings of groups of like-minded people can be of great help in trying out your ideas and capitalize on the positive feedback, that such communities will offer as you explore your unique contributions. Don't look at your gifts as the things that you do in your spare time, but rather as the things that are part of the purpose of your life. This will assist you in shifting to the prosperity consciousness where your gifts are viewed as the resource that is of value to you and the community.

Last but not least, when you are still in the process of searching for yourself and your talents, you can always think about how those skills can be applied in the business model. What can you do to ensure that your talents are put to work in a way that satisfies your audience's demands while also fulfilling your soul? This alignment not only increases your satisfaction but also allows you to connect with clients who appreciate your message. This way, you imbue your business with your talents and build a meaningful way to achieve success that reflects both your soul and business journey combined.

Creating a Business that Reflects Your Soul's Purpose

Building a business that is an extension of your soul's purpose is a liberating process that calls you to integrate your life's work with your spirit's calling. For you, this alignment is not just a business decision; it is an invitation to share an expression of your essence and a way to contribute to the collective consciousness. The process begins with self-assessment as one learns his or her strengths, interests and talents. Building a business that you are aligned with at core level is essential for creating one that resonates with your true self and fulfills your spiritual mission.

To embark on this journey, it is vital to cultivate mindfulness and awareness. Engage in practices that allow you to connect with your inner self, such as meditation, journaling, or nature walks. These practices help you to continuously clarify your vision and intentions. As you develop a deeper understanding of your soul's purpose, you can begin to articulate how this purpose translates into a business model. Consider the impact you wish to have on others and the legacy you want to create. This vision will serve as your guiding star, helping you navigate challenges and opportunities along your entrepreneurial path.

There are others whose soul's purpose is to assist you in discovering your own. One of the ways is through spiritual coaching which helps to identify and maintain your path to your life's purpose. Bear in mind that you develop subjective perception of reality and another's opinion can provide you with more information that you would not be able to receive on your own. When you can release the need to be right, or the belief that it must be done in a specific manner, your soul's mission has the chance to be the motivating force.

Knowing the soul's purpose, the next thing that comes into mind is how to infuse it into the business. This means developing a business model that is not only the commercial model but also the moral model, the efficient model, and the proper model for society. Soul-centered entrepreneurship helps you create a business that is aligned with your values, where you can offer products or services, or interact with clients based on your purpose. When you bring legitimacy and intentionality into your business, you draw people who believe in your cause and help you build a community around that cause.

Last but not least, spiritual practices are the best way towards having a work-life which enables the balance between your business and your soul purpose. One can easily get lost in the hustle of running a business and it is only when you get a reminder in the form of a spiritual practice that you are reminded of why you are doing it. From yoga to mindfulness to taking breaks to do things for self-care, these things keep you grounded and focused. The bonus for you is that as you respect your energy, you build a healthy business model that supports your soul's vision and allows for a prosperous sustainable entrepreneurial experience.

CHAPTER 5

Energy Healing for Business Professionals

Understanding Energy Dynamics in Business

Energy dynamics in business can be defined as the forces that exist in an organization that drive how energy flows through creativity, motivation, and productivity. Energy is like the lifeblood of the universe and the same principle applies to a business; a business's energy permeates through all the activities, interactions, decisions, and results. To the spiritual seeker and the new economy entrepreneur, it is important to understand these dynamics not only as a route to the accumulation of money but, as a way of creating a business environment that is in harmony with a higher purpose. If you understand the vibrations that are present within a business environment, it is possible to create a harmonious work environment that will resonate with spiritual aspirations.

In energy dynamics, the fundamental law is vibration. Each and every single idea, feeling, and activity send out a vibration that can raise or lower the consciousness of a company. All spiritual teachings encourage you to stay in high vibration. Within a company, this entails developing a positive organizational culture, promoting open and honest communication and making sure that energies generated within the organization are in harmony with the mission and vision of the organization. When you rise up your own vibration, you improve your efficiency and create a positive environment for everyone around you to grow.

When it comes to connecting your business with your soul's purpose, energy dynamics will be very important. You can improve the vibrational frequency of your company and raise your own vibration by implementing energy practices like Reiki, crystal healing, sound therapy, or other forms of energy healing. This comprehensive approach promotes abundance and positivity, creating harmony for you, your clients, and other team members. As you work on this energetic alignment, you may also find that your intuition gets better, which will help you make decisions that are entirely in harmony with the purpose of your soul.

Mindfulness-based business strategies also play a crucial role in managing energy dynamics. By incorporating practices such as meditation, breathwork, and conscious reflection into daily routines, you can cultivate self-awareness and emotional intelligence. This heightened awareness allows you to observe your thoughts and feelings without judgment, facilitating a clearer understanding of how your energy impacts the workplace. Being more attuned to your energy, you can better navigate interpersonal relationships and conflicts, leading to a more cohesive and resilient business dynamic.

A soul-centered business journey challenges you to bring your essence into your business activities. Your energy and how you manage it creates this essence. Using a Soulful Success approach, you must look at the fact that companies are more than just profit-making machines; they are also tools for individual and group change. You can generate positive energy dynamics that draw fulfillment and prosperity by coordinating your business objectives with your spiritual beliefs. For example, when a business professional places a high priority on social responsibility, ethical behavior, and community involvement, it creates a positive vibe that appeals to stakeholders and customers, which eventually results in increased success and loyalty.

Finally, it's vital to understand that managing energy dynamics will mean continuous professional and personal growth. It's important to regularly evaluate your objectives and how they match your spiritual path so you can modify your tactics as necessary as you grow and your energy changes. In addition to encouraging work-life balance, this practice or periodic reassessment, cultivates a sense of fulfillment that goes beyond financial gain. You can continue building business that is fueled by genuineness, connection, and a common vision of abundance by adopting the idea of energy dynamics. This will make the path to Soulful Success both enlightening and life-changing.

Techniques for Energy Clearing and Balancing

For all business professionals, especially spiritual seekers and business owner, energy clearing and balancing are crucial practices to foster a peaceful environment that supports professional and personal development. Keeping a clear and balanced energy field can greatly improve decision-making, creativity, and general well-being in the business world where stress and distractions are commonplace. You should incorporate the energy clearing and balancing techniques covered in this subchapter into your daily routines and business plans.

<u>Visualization:</u>

Of the many techniques of energy clearing, visualization is one of the most efficient.

EXERCISE -

Picture a bright cleansing light enveloping you, and your working environment.

See it penetrating every corner of your workspace and penetrating all of you, top to bottom.

As you visualize this light, focus on releasing any negative energy, stress, or emotional blockages. Keep your focus on the feeling of peace and tranquility as the light fills you and your workspace.

This visualization exercise can be a part of your morning routine to set a positive tone for your day. This practice not only helps to clear your energy but also promotes a sense of calm and clarity for the day, allowing you to approach your business activities with renewed focus and intention.

<u>Grounding:</u>

Another strong energy balancing method is the method of grounding. Grounding techniques anchor you to the earth's energy thus assisting in balancing your emotional and energy bodies. Some of these activities include: going for a walk without shoes and socks, sitting under a tree, or entertaining a nature meditation. A good exercise for grounding is connecting with earth's energy by visualizing roots into the earth.

EXERCISE – (you may want to record for yourself)

Grounding Exercise: "Extending Roots into the Earth"

1. Get into a comfortable position while standing or sitting, keeping your feet planted firmly on the ground.
2. Close your eyes and take a few deep breaths, inhaling deeply and exhaling slowly. Let your body relax with each breath.
3. Quiet your mind and focus on setting the intention for grounding into earth while balancing your energy. Intend on releasing stress, gaining clarity, or simply feeling more present.
4. Imagine that roots are growing from the soles of your feet. These roots start small, but as you focus on them, they grow thicker and longer, extending deep into the earth beneath you.
5. Picture the roots reaching further and further down, passing through layers of soil, rock, and mineral. Feel the strength and support of the earth as your roots continue to grow.
6. Once your roots are firmly anchored deep within the earth, imagine pulling up the earth's nourishing energy through your roots. Visualize this energy as a warm, golden light flowing up from the earth, through your roots, into your feet, and gradually spreading throughout your body.
7. As you receive the earth's grounding energy, let go of any tension, stress, or negative energy. Visualize it flowing out of your body, down through your roots, and being absorbed and transformed by the earth.

8. With each breath, feel more centered, present, and connected to the earth. Let this grounded feeling support you as you move forward with your day.
9. After a few minutes, begin to slowly bring your awareness back to your body. Wiggle your toes and fingers, and when you're ready, open your eyes.

This exercise will greatly reinforce grounding your energy. When your energy is centered and connected, it becomes easier to navigate the challenges of entrepreneurship, making decisions that align with your true purpose and values.

<u>Sound:</u>

It is also possible to use sound as a method of energy clearing and balancing. This technique can involve using sound frequencies like singing bowls, chimes, tuning forks or even your own voice. Sound can move energy around to change any stagnant energy. Music would fall into this category as well and we all know how music can change a mood!

Sound healing works by sending sound waves through the body and surrounding space allowing the release of negative emotions and promoting positive energy flow. Practicing sound healing on a weekly basis will improve your energetic wellbeing, helping you to attract abundance while fostering fulfillment because you are in alignment with your soul purpose.

<u>Mindfulness:</u>

Finally, it is possible to use mindful rituals to complement your regular activities, which will greatly improve the overall effectiveness of energy-cleansing and energizing techniques.

Small things can be mindful activities like lighting a candle, burning sage, using some essential oils... all help create a sacred space that will promote positive energy and a sense of peace and clarity.

Setting a timer to remind you to pause and reflect can go a long way in balancing your energy.

Incorporating any mindful rituals should serve as a reminder to pause and reconnect to you purpose which will refocus your energy. When your energy is focused on your purpose and why you are in business, you can easily release any negative energy of overwhelm or anxiety. This way, you create an environment that fosters your spiritual self and your business goals, hence a more enriching business experience.

The Impact of Energy on Business Relationships

The dynamics of our business relationships and the overall success of any business endeavors are significantly impacted by the energy we bring to the table. It is also important to look at collective energy because understanding energy as both a personal and collective force will help you find their way to more meaningful and profound connections on your business journey. Consider that energy, in this context, refers not only to our personal vibrations but also to the collective energies that arise in group settings, meetings, and partnerships. Your understanding and awareness of these energies can foster environments where authenticity, collaboration, and mutual growth can thrive.

Mindfulness will always play a pivotal role in shaping the energy we put forth and receive within our business relationships. When you practice mindfulness, you become more attuned to your thoughts, feelings, and intentions, leading to clearer communication and more harmonious interactions. This heightened awareness also allows for the identification of energy leaks—those moments when negativity or stress disrupts the flow of collaboration. By addressing these leaks through practices such as meditation, breathwork, or simply pausing to reflect, you can realign your energies, creating a nurturing space for creativity and innovation.

Furthermore, remember the idea of energy healing will not just greatly improve business relationships but also your personal well-being. As previously addressed, the use of energy healing like Reiki, chakra balancing, and other healing modalities to raise you own vibration also has a positive impact on the overall energy of your workplace. This ripple effect fosters a culture of support and openness, empowering those you encounter to also work together with you more effectively toward shared goals.

Recognizing and utilizing energy becomes crucial in the context of Soulful Success in order to match personal values with business goals. When the needs of the market collide with their inner calling, spiritual seekers frequently find themselves at a crossroads. Spiritual practices can help you find the energies that align with your basic beliefs by emphasizing energy alignment. In addition to increasing personal fulfillment, this alignment draws in clients and like-minded partners, resulting in more satisfying business partnerships based on a common goal.

In the end, it is impossible to undervalue the influence of energy on business relationships. The energies we exchange and embody have a profound impact on how we interact, negotiate, and work together. While keeping an open mind to comprehend the energies of others, spiritual seekers are urged to develop a profound awareness of their own energetic presence. You can build strong, enduring relationships that propel success and fulfillment in your business endeavors by incorporating this energetic wisdom into routine business procedures. In addition to changing people's experiences, this all-encompassing strategy can help the world move toward more ethical and caring business practices.

CHAPTER 6

Finding Your Purpose

Discovering Your Life Purpose

Discovering one's calling is widely explained as a process rather than an event. Life after all is about the journey, not the destination. In the spiritual path to self-realization in the business and personal development arenas, discovering your life's calling; your very purpose for being here, is a liberating process that impacts everything you experience. This discovery leads to a wonderful integration between your inner world and the outer reality. You will discover a path that not only fosters your own fulfillment but also increases your influence on the world when you incorporate spiritual wisdom into your business endeavors.

In order to start this process of discovering yourself, there is one applicable rule: be mindful and be aware. This includes listening to your feelings – your heart, and being able to pick signs to discern that you are indeed on the right path.

EXERCISE –

Exercise for Life Purpose Journaling

Locate a peaceful area where you won't be bothered for at least twenty to thirty minutes.

Make a conscious effort to access your inner wisdom.

Answer the following questions as you see fit, without giving them too much thought. Allow your mind to wander:

Journal Prompt:

Which pursuits make me feel the happiest and most fulfilled?

When do I feel most alive and genuine?

If I knew I couldn't fail, what would I do?

What would I do with my life if I had limitless resources, money, and time?

Why and who do I admire? (What traits or behaviors in other people motivate you?)

Find recurring themes in your responses. Emphasize or circle words or concepts that are used repeatedly. These will assist you in identifying *your basic beliefs and aspirations.*

Now try and create a purpose statement by using the themes and insights you've gathered. Try to complete the sentence: "My life purpose is to... (help, create, guide, inspire) because I value..."

When thinking about your purpose, it is crucial to recognize that your purpose often extends beyond mere personal achievement. This means you should not narrowly define your purpose solely in terms of your self-interest however... you need to understand that your purpose goes beyond the desire to achieve. It is naturally connected to what you do to other people and the difference you can make in your community and the whole world. Soulful Success inspires you to see commerce as a means of giving voice to your values and creating a positive change. This entails incorporating compassion and mindfulness into your business plans to make sure that your work supports your spiritual convictions and improves the lives of others.

Remember to embrace energy healing techniques previously learned, because they can also facilitate the discovery and ongoing expression of your life purpose. By looking at your energy and understanding what energetic dynamics are at play during your business journey, you can begin to identify blockages that may be holding you back. Energy healing practices can help you clear these obstacles, allowing for a more authentic expression of your purpose. This holistic approach not only helps you to connect with your inner self but also fosters a sense of balance and alignment in your work-life dynamic, essential for sustainable success.

Ultimately, discovering your life purpose is about embracing the journey of growth and transformation. It requires a willingness to explore, reflect, and engage with your inner wisdom while remaining open to the possibilities that lie ahead. By integrating spiritual practices into your life and business, you create a framework through which to manifest your dreams and aspirations while honoring your purpose. As you align your actions with your purpose, you will find that success is not merely measured by external achievements but by the fulfillment and joy that arise from living authentically and serving your community with love and intention.

Aligning Goals with Spiritual Aspirations

Aligning business or career goals with spiritual aspirations is essential for those seeking a holistic approach to success. In the fast-paced world of business, it's easy to become disconnected from the core values and spiritual purpose that drove you to pursue your business in the first place. For you, finding a balance between professional ambitions and spiritual growth not only enhances personal fulfillment but also fosters a more profound impact on the world. We will explore the process of consciously integrating your spiritual beliefs and values into your business or career objectives, offering practical insights for a fulfilling business journey.

Firstly, it's important to clarify your spiritual goals going forward. What are your ideas for growing? This could involve activities like meditation, spending time in nature on a regular basis, or maybe being dedicated to serving others and engaging with the community. By expressing these goals clearly, you establish a guiding light that can steer your personal journey. Having this clarity helps you evaluate opportunities and make sure they fit well with your purpose. For instance, if service to others is an ongoing spiritual aspiration, consider how your business can incorporate acts of kindness, mentorship, or community engagement, ensuring that your daily work reflects your spiritual mission.

Next, think about this transformative strategy that challenges you to assess not only your business goals but also your motivations for pursuing them. You can find deeper motivations and intentions behind your business goals by journaling and practicing self-reflection. Finding the "why" behind your goals will help you match your spiritual purpose with your career goals because it guarantees that your work speaks to both your inner self and your outward goals. This alignment generates a synergistic energy that can help you advance both personally and professionally.

EXERCISE –

Finding the "why" behind aspirations is essential for aligning goals with deeper personal meaning to align them with your spiritual aspirations. Here's a structured process you can follow to uncover the "why" behind your aspirations:

1. Start by clearly defining your aspiration. What is the goal or desire you're aiming for? Whether it's a professional goal, a personal achievement, or a lifestyle change, articulate it clearly.

Example: "I want to start my own business."

2. Ask yourself why you want to achieve this aspiration. Your first answer may be surface-level, but it will open up the exploration process.

Example: "Why do I want to start my own business? Because I want to be my own boss."

3. Use the "5 Whys" technique to dig deeper into your motivations. After each answer, ask "Why?" again to push beyond superficial reasoning.

Example:

- Why do you want to be your own boss? "So I can have more control over my schedule."
- Why do you want more control over your schedule? "So I can spend more time with my family."
- Why is spending more time with your family important? "Because I feel like I'm missing out on their lives with my current job."
- Why is that a concern for you? "Because I value deep connections and quality time with my loved ones."
- Why is that a key value? "Because family is what makes me feel most fulfilled and supported."

4. Through the "5 Whys" exercise, you'll likely start identifying deeper core values. These values could include things like freedom, security, connection, love, or creativity. These are the driving forces behind your aspirations.

   Example: From the exploration above, the core value behind wanting to start a business might be "family connection" or "fulfillment through relationships."

5. Notice what emotions arise when you think about your aspiration and its deeper purpose.

   Does it bring feelings of joy, excitement, peace, or passion?

   These emotions will show how connected you are to your "why." As you ensure your "why" feels authentic to you and not influenced by external pressures or societal expectations.

Ask yourself: Am I pursuing this goal for me, or is this driven by someone else's idea of success?

Example: You may realize that your desire to start a business is not just about financial success, but about creating a lifestyle that aligns with your personal values and what truly matters to you.

6. Now that you've uncovered the deeper "why," refine your aspiration to be more aligned with it. This could involve rethinking the original goal or adjusting it to better fit the purpose you've discovered.

   Example: Instead of just wanting to "start a business," your aspiration might evolve into "start a business that allows for flexible hours so I can prioritize family time."

Mindfulness-based business strategies can also play a crucial role in this alignment. By being mindful and staying present in the moment at work and in decision making processes you can understand how your choices affect your spiritual aspirations. Integrating mindfulness practices, like breathing or taking breaks during your day can assist you in navigating the intricate landscape of the business realm while staying connected to your spiritual core. Engaging in this habit not only improves your judgment skills., but also cultivates a feeling of calm and understanding while helping you stay connected to your chosen spiritual aspirations.

Lastly, incorporating energy healing practices can enhance the harmony between business objectives and spiritual goals. By utilizing energy healing methods one can remove obstacles that might block advancement or create conflict between their business journey and spiritual beliefs. Practices, like Reiki, aligning chakras and even guided imagery can assist in sustaining an energy state that allows for the attraction of opportunities that are fully aligned. By embracing energy strategies and principles in your life, you can help create a conscious blend between your work and spiritual pursuits that can lead to a deeper sense of satisfaction and achievement in the long run.

Strategies for Purpose-Driven Development

In the evolving world of business today the key to satisfaction and prosperity lies in connecting your business journey with a deeper sense of purpose and meaning that speaks to your true self. You do this by infusing spiritual elements into your professional endeavors. This goes beyond the usual strategies for advancing in business by integrating mindfulness practices that aligns energy flow towards achieving abundance goals that bring both success in the usual sense yet fulfillment at a deeper personal level.

Self-reflection and mindfulness exercises are useful methods for this kind of growth. You can gain clarity on the path your business journey should take by taking the time to understand your core values, passions, and strengths. Journaling and meditation are examples of mindfulness exercises that help you calm your mind and connect with your inner wisdom, which can lead to insights that can create informed business decisions. You can make well-informed decisions about your future course by routinely evaluating how your current business aligns with your values and purpose. This will ensure that your work supports your personal development and contributions to the world.

Another key strategy is the cultivation of a supportive network that aligns with your spiritual and business aspirations. Surrounding oneself with like-minded individuals can foster an environment of encouragement and inspiration. This network could include mentors, fellow spiritual practitioners, and professionals in the same field who share a commitment to purpose-driven practices in business. Engaging in communities, whether online or in person, dedicated to both a spiritual life and business growth can facilitate collaboration and idea exchange, allowing individuals to learn from one another's experiences and collectively elevate their business journey.

Also, keep in mind, as stated before, your business development can be improved by incorporating energy healing techniques into your business development. Energy techniques like Reiki or chakra balancing can assist in removing obstacles that impede business expansion and address self-doubt. You can develop a more assured and powerful presence in your work life by tackling these energetic obstacles. In addition to fostering personal wellbeing, this energy alignment helps to draw opportunities that are in line with your purpose, making it easier for you to create the results you want.

Lastly, a visionary approach to business planning is crucial for those seeking purpose-driven business development. Setting intentions that reflect your spiritual beliefs and business aspirations can help guide decision-making and strategic planning. This could include creating a vision board that incorporates both professional goals and spiritual values so you have a daily reminder of your intended purpose. It's a reminder that by integrating spiritual frameworks into business strategies you can develop a holistic plan that not only drives financial success but also nurtures your soul. Ultimately, these strategies empower you to navigate your business journey with intention, authenticity, and a profound sense of purpose.

EXERCISE –

If you've never made a vision board here's how:

1. Spend some time thinking about the things you wish to bring into your life before you begin.

Put specific goals or desires in writing, whether they have to do with your relationships, career, health, or personal development.

Think about all of your desires without filters.

The way you want to feel after achieving your goals is just as important as the "things" you desire.

2. Collect Supplies

- A corkboard or poster board: Select a surface that appeals to you.
- Digital boards (Canva, Pinterest) are preferred by some, but physical boards facilitate greater interaction.
- Look for magazines and printable images on the internet. Think of images that best reflect your objectives then cut them out.
- Find affirmations and quotes that uplift you and support your goals.
- Gather any additional materials you might need to customize your board, such as scissors, glue, and stickers.

3. You can lay out your sections before attaching them Your vision board can be arranged according to various aspects of your life, including:

- Career and business
- Family and relationships
- Personal development
- Spiritual growth
- Health and wellness
- Finances

4. Put your board together

- As you arrange the pictures, picture yourself with these items already in your life
- Add a personal touch by including pictures of yourself, particularly from successful or joyful times. This makes it easier for you to feel the energy of your objectives.
- Make it beautiful. You'll feel more inspired if it's visually appealing.

Once you're done, place your vision board somewhere you'll see it every day, such as your bedroom or office. This continuous reminder keeps you inspired and committed to your goals.

CHAPTER 7

Manifestation and Abundance

The Principles of Manifestation

Understanding how to match the realities of your external environment with your inner desires is based on the principles of manifestation. When it comes to the idea of "Soulful Success," these ideas act as a link between spiritual wisdom and real-world business application. Manifesting is not just about wishing for outcomes, it requires a deeper understanding of how intention, belief, and action all work together. When you learn how to understand and then embrace these principles you can navigate your business with better clarity and purpose, thereby ensuring your business ventures align with your core beliefs.

The principle of intention is central to manifestation. At its core, intention is not just a passing idea, but a concentrated dedication to a particular goal, in order to achieve a specific result. Setting precise intentions helps you make a plan that directs your choices and activities. When you have clarity on your intentions, your energies will be more in line with your objectives, making it easier to identify opportunities you have otherwise not seen, or just ignored. You can develop a mindset that is open to new opportunities and abundance by consistently practicing intention-setting. This will enable you to draw in the connections and resources required to thrive.

Belief is another important principle. Our reality is shaped by our beliefs, which also serve as the catalyst for our intentions to become reality in the field of manifestation. When you have limiting ideas about your abilities or worthiness, it can lead to energetic roadblocks that stop your progress. On the other hand, when you nurture empowering beliefs, like self-value and abundance, it can significantly change how you perceive things around you. It's important to look at changing your limiting beliefs, whether you do it through visualization, affirmations, or energy healing techniques, you can strengthen a positive mindset that will help you on your path to abundance and manifestation.

The third principle of manifestation is action, which acts as a link between reality and intention. While ideas and convictions are important, visions cannot be realized without concrete actions. Being proactive and receptive to the intuitive cues that appear along the business path are necessary for this. Since mindfulness-based business strategies promote a balanced approach to decision-making and action, they can be extremely helpful in this situation. Being conscious and in the moment allows you to determine which actions are in line with both your business objectives and your soul's purpose, making every action significant and effective.

Finally, the principle of gratitude amplifies the manifestation process. When gratitude is practiced, it creates a positive feedback loop that will enhance your energy. By acknowledging and appreciating the abundance that already exists in your life and business, you can attract even more of what you desire. This principle is especially powerful in business, where the energy of appreciation can foster stronger relationships with clients, collaborators, and with the community. Cultivating a practice of gratitude not only enriches personal experiences but also elevates the overall vibrational frequency of a business, paving the way for greater success and fulfillment. By integrating these principles of manifestation, you can embark on a journey that harmonizes your aspirations with your spiritual path, leading to your Soulful Success.

Overcoming Limiting Beliefs

Overcoming limiting beliefs is a crucial step in the journey toward Soulful Success, especially for spiritual seekers who are navigating and integrating the complex realms of business and personal growth. Limiting beliefs are often deeply ingrained thought patterns that can restrict your potential and influence your actions. They may stem from past experiences, societal expectations, or even well-meaning advice from peers and mentors. Recognizing and dismantling these beliefs is essential for anyone looking to integrate spiritual wisdom into their business practices and cultivate a life of abundance and fulfillment.

In order to kickstart this journey effectively it's crucial to pinpoint those beliefs that are holding you back from moving forward. Take time for self-reflection through activities like writing in a journal or practicing meditation to delve into the stories you might have adopted about money, achievement and your own skills. Asking yourself questions such as "What are my thoughts, about prosperity?". How do I see my value in the business world?" can assist in revealing the beliefs that no longer support your growth. As you become aware of these beliefs. Bring them into the discussion with yourself or others around you. You can then start questioning their truth and delving into viewpoints that resonate better with your identified principles and goals.

Changing your perspective to one of abundance and possibility is a powerful way to overcome limiting beliefs. In this context, mindfulness-based techniques like affirmations and visualization can be especially beneficial. Imagine yourself reaching your objectives and becoming the successful person you want to be and think about how that will feel. By substituting positive statements for negative self-talk, affirmations can support this new way of thinking. You can change your focus from scarcity to abundance and take control of the concept of abundance by telling yourself, for instance, "I am worthy of success, and abundance flows to me effortlessly."

Building a support network around you are crucial when tackling your self-imposed beliefs that hold you back in life. Interact with individuals and experts who resonate with your values and dreams. Engaging with people who share interests and values can be truly motivating whether it's through attending workshops or networking events or even interacting in online communities. These connections can act as a source of motivation and encouragement by showing you your strengths and capabilities beyond what you might have thought possible on your own. Also, having peers to hold you accountable and offer support can greatly boost your efforts in confronting and changing any self-imposed restrictions and can assist you in creating new empowering affirmations for yourself.

Ultimately, overcoming limiting beliefs is not a one-time event but an ongoing journey that requires commitment and practice. The outcome though is that as you continue to refine your mindset and align your actions with your spiritual principles, you will likely find new opportunities and pathways unfold before you. Embrace this process of self-discovery and growth, and remember that every step you take toward releasing limiting beliefs is a step toward a more fulfilling and purpose-driven life. The bonus will be that by integrating spiritual wisdom into your business journey, you not only pave the way for your own success but also inspire others to embark on their transformative journeys as well.

Practical Steps to Attract Abundance

Both an individual and an organization can ascribe to a mindset of abundance by consciously aligning intentions, beliefs and actions. This journey begins with self-awareness, because understanding your current mindset is crucial. Start assessing your ideas regarding money, success and your own worthiness. Consider that your limiting beliefs or negative thought patterns have been unconsciously shaping your financial realities.

This is where journaling can prove to be particularly helpful in expressing and reviewing your current beliefs and recognizing fears, hidden doubts or thoughts that could otherwise get in the way of the abundance you seek. These beliefs can be identified... which will allow you to shift toward a more empowering mindset.

Once you develop clarity with regard to your beliefs, it is important to never forget practicing the attitude of gratitude. Gratitude is a magnet for abundance; it changes your perspective from focusing on what is lacking in your life to what is already there. Begin every day by saying 'Thank you' for at least three things; they can include things, people or situations. This exercise not only enriches your emotional state, but sends out to the Universe a strong message that there is more to be received. By making this attitude of gratitude part of your daily activities, your view of life can be altered... which will lead to attracting more abundance.

Visualization is another powerful tool for attracting abundance. This practice involves creating a vivid mental image of your desired outcomes and embodying the feelings associated with achieving those goals. Spend a few minutes each day visualizing your success in specific areas of your life, such as your business or career, financial goals, or personal growth. Feel the emotions that come with these achievements—joy, satisfaction, and fulfillment. When you attach the emotion (energy in motion) to your desires, what you send out into the Universe becomes much more powerful. By consistently engaging in this practice, you also align your subconscious mind with your intentions, making it easier to know what action to take and thereby manifest those desires into reality. Remember that using vision boards can enhance your visualization practice, as they serve as tangible reminders of your goals and can inspire daily motivation.

It is important to always pay attention to your thoughts and feeling, because incorporating mindfulness into your business practices is essential for maintaining a sought after abundant and balanced mindset. Mindfulness encourages you to stay present, so it reduces anxiety about the future and regrets about the past. By grounding yourself in the present moment, you can make more conscious decisions that align with your values and purpose. This practice can be as simple as taking a few deep breaths before meetings or setting aside time for meditation each day. Mindfulness not only enhances your decision-making abilities but also invites clarity and creativity into your work, allowing for innovative solutions that will attract abundance.

Lastly, the same as overcoming limiting beliefs, surround yourself with a supportive community that resonates with your spiritual and abundance goals. Engaging with like-minded individuals can provide encouragement, inspiration, and accountability on your abundance journey. Sharing experiences and wisdom within a supportive network fosters a sense of belonging and will amplify your abundance mindset.

By following these practical steps, you will develop a stronger bond with your purpose and spiritual core in addition to drawing abundance into your life.

CHAPTER 8

Work-Life Balance through Spiritual Practices

Understanding the Importance of Balance

In the fast-paced world of business, especially for you if you are a spiritual seeker, finding balance becomes not only a personal endeavor but also a professional necessity. Balance is the foundation upon which any sustainable success is built. It involves harmonizing various aspects of life—emotional, physical, mental, and spiritual—to create an environment conducive to growth and fulfillment. When balance is achieved you can navigate the complexities of business with a clear mind and a grounded spirit, allowing you to remain focused on your purpose while also being responsive to the needs of your business.

From a spiritual perspective, balance is essential for maintaining your energy and vitality. Entrepreneurs and business professionals often experience the dual pressures of ambition and responsibility, which can lead to burnout if not managed effectively. Mindfulness practices will play a vital role in cultivating this balance, enabling you to stay present and centered amidst any chaos. By integrating mindfulness-based strategies into your daily routine you can create a buffer against stress, enhancing your ability to make sound decisions and connect more deeply with your clients or business associates.

Keep in mind that achieving Soulful Success necessitates making a deliberate effort to match your business operations with your spiritual principles and basic values. You will eventually create an atmosphere that encourages creativity and intuition which will produce more creative solutions and services as a result of this alignment. Prioritizing balance will help you focus your energies more effectively on

57

worthwhile endeavors that support your mission. In addition to drawing wealth, this alignment fosters a sense of fulfillment that goes beyond material success, thereby fulfilling your soul in the process.

Understanding the significance of balance in business also requires an understanding of work-life balance. Many business professionals are caught in the vicious cycle of working too much out of passion and disregarding their own health. Restoring balance through the integration of spiritual practices into daily life can free up time for family, community, and self-care. In addition to improving personal fulfillment, this all-encompassing strategy boosts business performance because a refreshed body and mind foster increased creativity and productivity.

In the end, finding balance is a dynamic process that calls for constant introspection and modification. Visionary business planning that incorporates a spiritual framework encourages you to evaluate how well your strategies align with your core values on a regular basis. You can create a more harmonious life that supports your personal and professional goals by regularly assessing your physical, emotional, and spiritual well-being. You can create a prosperous and fulfilling business journey that promotes a life of abundance, joy, and purpose by cultivating this understanding of balance.

This holistic approach not only improves personal satisfaction but also boosts business performance because a refreshed body and mind lead to more creativity and productivity.

Spiritual Practices for Soulful Success

Spiritual practices play a crucial role in fostering "Soulful Success" particularly when you seek to harmonize your personal values with your professional endeavors. In the context of "Soulful Success," these practices can be integrated into various aspects of business and entrepreneurship, allowing you to cultivate a deeper connection with your work and the world around you. By embracing mindfulness, intention, and energy awareness you can create a business environment that not only supports your financial objectives but also aligns with your spiritual beliefs and environmental responsibilities.

Mindfulness should be viewed as a part of anyone's spiritual journey. While your spiritual journey is unique to you, mindfulness-based strategies are essential for maintaining clarity and focus in a fast-paced business world. As you should know by now practicing mindfulness involves being fully present in the moment, which can enhance decision-making and reduce stress. Being in the present moment allows your spiritual values to come into play, and this will encourage thoughtful action rather than reactive behavior.

Another reminder here is that energy healing is a powerful tool for staying spiritually connected. By understanding and managing your energy, you can reconnect to your core values and soul's calling while you navigate the challenges of business with greater ease. Use the techniques that you have found will best promote a sense of balance and harmony. These practices not only benefit you but also create a ripple effect that positively influences all aspects of your business day.

You should always be inspired by your spiritual practices to match your business goals with your innermost beliefs and desires. Examining your life's purpose and how it relates to your business endeavors is always beneficial. because this alignment fosters a sense of fulfillment that go beyond conventional ideas of success.

In order to develop workable plans that lead you to significant results, keep in mind to set clear intentions and use reflective activities like journaling or vision boarding. In addition to improving individual satisfaction, this process helps create a more ethical and sustainable business environment.

Finally, achieving work-life balance through spiritual practices is essential for sustaining long-term success. Incorporating rituals such as gratitude journaling, nature walks, or digital detoxes can help you recharge and reconnect with your inner self. These practices not only improve personal well-being but also enhance productivity and creativity in any workplace. By prioritizing self-care and spiritual growth, you can cultivate a harmonious relationship between your professional responsibilities and personal life. Ultimately, integrating spiritual practices into sustainable living creates a holistic approach that nurtures both you and the larger community, paving the way for a more conscious and compassionate business world.

Creating Boundaries for Spiritual and Professional Growth

Creating boundaries is an essential practice for anyone on a path of spiritual and business growth, particularly for spiritual seekers and entrepreneurs. Boundaries serve as a protective framework that allows you to protect and cultivate your energy, maintain focus, and align your actions with your core values. Establishing boundaries can help to prevent burnout, foster healthier relationships, and create space for positive development. By understanding the significance of boundaries, you can more effectively navigate the challenges of integrating your inner wisdom with your business ambitions.

The understanding that energy is a limited resource is fundamental to setting boundaries. This knowledge is essential for anyone who is a spiritual entrepreneur, works in energy healing, or is a spiritual seeker in the workplace. Energy is needed for every interaction, task, and commitment, and it is easy to run out of it in the absence of boundaries. Decreased creativity, irritability, or even a break from your spiritual practice are some of the ways that this depletion can show up. You can prioritize your energy and make sure that it is going toward endeavors that support both your business and spiritual goals by establishing boundaries.

Mindfulness-based business strategies emphasize the importance of your self-awareness in creating boundaries. Practicing mindfulness allows you to tune into your thoughts, emotions, and physical sensations, providing insight into when boundaries are being crossed. For instance, a spiritual entrepreneur may notice feelings of overwhelm during client interactions or a lack of motivation for certain tasks, signaling a need for boundaries. By paying attention to these signals, you can take proactive steps to protect your time and energy, whether that means saying no to certain commitments or designating specific times for self-care and reflection. This mindfulness approach to setting boundaries not only helps maintain personal balance but also enhances professional effectiveness.

Boundaries are also essential for creating positive relationships with clients and coworkers for soul-centered entrepreneurship. Mutual respect can be established while misunderstandings can be avoided with clear communication regarding availability, expectations, and limits. Setting boundaries creates a positive, healthy dynamic that inspires your clients or coworkers to follow suit. Consequently, this leads to a more sustainable business approach that honors both your professional and spiritual aspects. Setting boundaries will give you the freedom to be who you truly are and interact with people in a meaningful way.

Last but not least, the concepts of abundance and manifestation are closely aligned to the practice of establishing boundaries. A roadmap for your spiritual and business journeys is created when you identify what you need and want. On this journey, boundaries act as markers, directing choices and actions that result in increased fulfillment. You can draw in opportunities that align with your goals and values by stating your personal and professional boundaries clearly. By clearly articulating personal and professional limits, you will be more likely to attract opportunities that resonate with your values and intentions. This holistic approach ensures that as you strive for success, you do so in a way that honors your spiritual journey and contributes positively to your overall well-being.

CHAPTER 9

Visionary Business Planning with a Spiritual Framework

Integrating Spirituality into Business Planning

Bringing spirituality into the realm of business planning can be a game changer as it merges your essence with the initiatives of your company. This integration serves as a roadmap for achieving success in a way that genuinely reflects your values and beliefs. By infusing spiritual concepts into your business structure you create a workspace where both purpose and profit can thrive together in harmony and enrich your experiences significantly.

Achieving constant clarity of purpose is a crucial component of incorporating spirituality into business planning. Spiritual seekers must always identify their "why" to uncover the driving forces behind their company. This calls for in-depth self-reflection to reveal the motivations behind your business. When you align your vision with a purpose that reflects your spiritual path, it becomes a guiding force for your decisions and a source of inspiration for others. This clarity increases the positive effects of your business by attracting like-minded customers and partners as well as fostering a sense of community and shared values.

When it comes to incorporating spirituality into your business strategy and planning, your mindfulness exercises will play a key role. You can stay in the moment and be aware of the energies at work in your business. By making decisions mindfully, you are able to make better decisions, handle difficulties gracefully, and keep a balanced viewpoint thanks to this awareness. This also helps you improve your intuition and make sure that your actions are in line with your spiritual values and vision. Mindfulness exercises like breathwork, meditation, or reflective journaling should be a part of your business routine.

The idea of energy alignment in your business is another important component of this integration. You can approach opportunities and challenges in a completely different way if you realize that your business is an extension of your own energy. You can improve your creative flow, remove obstacles, and draw abundance by using energy healing techniques. In addition to helping you, this energetic alignment has a positive ripple effect on your business journey as it encourages a cooperative environment that thrives on respect and growth for all parties involved.

Last but not least, since your well-being has a direct impact on your business efficacy, preserving a work-life balance through spiritual practices is essential for long-term success. To revitalize your soul and stay in touch with your purpose, look at implementing spiritual rituals into your everyday schedule, such as nature walks or gratitude exercises. You can make sure that your business planning is about more than just financial metrics by making self-care and spiritual nourishment a priority. In the grand scheme of things, when it comes to business strategy and planning, it all boils down to achieving a fulfilling life where personal happiness and business accomplishments blend seamlessly together.

Setting Goals that Align with Your Soul's Vision

Setting goals that align with your soul's vision is a transformative process that goes beyond traditional planning methods. As a soul-centered entrepreneur when engaged in business understanding and expressing your soul's vision is essential for creating a roadmap that will resonate deeply with your core values and purpose. This alignment fosters not only personal fulfillment but also enhances your impact on the world. By crafting goals that reflect your true essence, you cultivate an environment where your business can thrive authentically, serving both your purpose and the needs of those you serve.

Start by taking some moments for yourself and really think about who you are and what matters most to you. This could involve meditation or simply jotting down your thoughts in a journal to connect with your true self and understand your values and dreams better. Consider what makes you happy and what kind of impact you want to leave on the world well.

When you think about what makes you happy as well as the impact you want to make, you start to imagine the bigger vision for yourself. This clear understanding is important since it serves as a guiding light, for your choices and behaviors. If you lack a grasp of your calling it can be difficult to establish goals that deeply connect with your greater mission. If you find yourself having trouble gaining clarity, consider seeking guidance from a a spiritual coach. You can also look at your soul matrix, akashic records, hand analysis, human design or any number of modalities available to help you open new understanding of self and your spiritual path.

Once you have a clear sense of your soul's vision, it's time to translate that vision into actionable goals. Use the SMART criteria—specific, measurable, achievable, relevant, and time-bound—as a framework, but infuse it with a spiritual lens. For example, while a goal may be to increase your client base, consider how this objective aligns with your desire to serve and uplift others. Ensure that each goal reflects your values and contributes to your overall vision, allowing you to operate not just from a place of ambition but from a space of soulful intention.

EXERCISE –

Setting goals that resonate with your authentic self involves a thoughtful process of self-reflection and alignment with your core values. Here's a structured approach to help you in this endeavor:

1. Self-Reflection

-   Make a list of your values (e.g., honesty, creativity, community, growth).
-   Reflect on your skills and what you enjoy doing. What activities make you feel alive and fulfilled?

2. Think About Your Future

-   Picture where you want to be in 5, 10, or 20 years. What does success look like for you?

3. Set Meaningful Goals

-   SMART Criteria: Ensure your goals are Specific, Measurable, Achievable, Relevant, and Time-bound.
-   Align with Values: Make sure each goal reflects your core values and passions. Ask yourself how achieving this goal will resonate with your authentic self.

4. Break Down Goals

-   Divide larger goals into smaller, manageable steps. This makes them less   overwhelming and more achievable.
-   Create milestones to track your progress. This can help you stay motivated and focused.

5. Create an Action Plan

-   Write down the specific actions you need to take for each goal. Include deadlines to create a sense of urgency.
-   Determine what resources or support you need to achieve your goals (e.g., mentors, books, courses).

Keep your mind open to how your journey may change as you set these goals. The path of a soul-centered professional or entrepreneur is rarely linear, and flexibility is key. Accept the idea that goals are not rigid endpoints but evolving signposts that can shift as your understanding of your soul's vision continues to expand. This flexibility enables you to gracefully handle new opportunities and difficulties keeping your business practices in line with your spiritual development. You can strengthen your connection to your purpose and improve your capacity to attract abundance by periodically reviewing and modifying your goals.

Lastly, use mindfulness-based techniques to keep your goals and soul journey in harmony. You can maintain your focus and sense of groundedness by regularly checking in with yourself, whether through visualization exercises, mindfulness exercises, or support from others. Developing an attitude of thankfulness for what is showing up can also help you become more conscious of how your life is progressing toward your objectives. You can strengthen the link between your actions and your soul's calling by recognizing and applauding small victories. This will help you strike a balance between your spiritual journey and your business goals.

Creating a Sustainable Business Model

Creating a sustainable business model is essential for anyone seeking to align professional endeavors with spiritual values. This means crafting a business that not only thrives financially but also nurtures the soul and contributes positively to the world. A sustainable business model transcends mere profitability; it embodies a commitment to ethical practices, social responsibility, and environmental stewardship. By integrating spiritual principles into every aspect of the business, you can create a model that resonates with your core beliefs and fosters a sense of purpose.

At the heart of a sustainable business model lies a clear mission statement that embodies your spiritual values and aspirations. This mission statement should explain not only what the company does, but also why it exists and the kind of impact it hopes to have on it's community and the world. Spiritual life and business coaches often emphasize the importance of this clarity, encouraging you to always tap into your inner wisdom to articulate your purpose. A mission that is imbued with spiritual intention acts as a beacon of light, directing decision-making and motivating you and your business ventures.

Creating a mission statement that reflects your spiritual values and aspirations is meaningful process that will continue to guide you.

EXERCISE –

1. First look back at previous exercises you did...

- Look at your core values and pinpoint those that resonate with your spiritual beliefs. (love, service, compassion, integrity, etc.)
- What is your ultimate purpose or calling?

2. Next, envision what your life looks like when you are living in alignment with your spiritual values. Ask yourself

- What impact do I want to make in this world?
- How do I want to feel?

3. Now, find your key themes or ideas from these reflections. It could be things like helping others, promoting peace, personal growth for self and others.

4. Draft Your Statement - Combine your values, purpose, and themes into a concise statement. Aim for clarity and authenticity. Start with a simple sentence or two, and then expand as needed. Use language that resonates with you and feels genuine. Avoid jargon or overly complex wording. You want a statement that is clear and easy to remember, typically 1-3 sentences long.

NOTE - As you share with others be open to feedback and consider revisions. Take time to revise until it feels right and evokes a sense of purpose and aligns with your spiritual path. Once you have a finalized statement, reflect on how it can influence your daily decisions and actions.

SAMPLES: Here are a few examples of mission statements that integrate spiritual values and aspirations:

1. Personal Growth and Service Mission Statement

"My mission is to live each day with compassion, love, and integrity, continuously growing in wisdom and understanding. I strive to use my spiritual gifts to uplift others and contribute to a more peaceful and just world."

2. Holistic Well-being and Empowerment Mission Statement

"I am committed to nurturing my body, mind, and spirit, aligning with my inner truth and divine purpose. My mission is to empower others to discover their own spiritual path and cultivate harmony within themselves and with the world around them."

3. Mindfulness and Connection Mission Statement

"My mission is to live in the present moment with mindfulness, gratitude, and peace. Through my spiritual practice, I seek to deepen my connection with others and the universe, creating spaces for healing and authentic connection."

4.. Community and Spiritual Leadership Mission Statement

"My mission is to serve as a compassionate leader and healer in my community, offering guidance and support to those seeking spiritual clarity. I aspire to embody unconditional love and wisdom, helping others connect with their higher selves and realize their full potential."

5. Environmental Stewardship and Spiritual Harmony Mission Statement

"I commit to living in harmony with the Earth, honoring all living beings as interconnected parts of the same spiritual whole. My mission is to protect the environment, promote sustainability, and inspire others to respect and care for our shared home."

Each example ties personal spiritual values, such as compassion, service, mindfulness, and growth, with aspirations like healing, empowerment, and leadership, creating a clear purpose that can guide daily actions and decisions.

Revisit your mission statement regularly to ensure it continues to resonate with your evolving spiritual journey. Consider incorporating it into your personal or professional spaces as a reminder of your commitment to living authentically.

When creating your sustainable business model, you should always practice being in the present moment, so that you can engage in more thoughtful and intentional actions. This approach fosters a culture of inclusivity and compassion and also allows you to stay attuned to your intuition, enabling you to adapt and pivot as necessary while remaining true to your core values. In this way, a sustainable business model not only supports financial viability but also enriches the human experience.

Soulful success emphasizes the importance of aligning business operations with spiritual principles, and this alignment can manifest in various ways throughout your business model. Consider sourcing materials ethically, implementing environmentally friendly practices, or practicing fair labor, whenever and wherever you can. This will coincide with your energy healing as ethical practices always help you maintain a higher vibration in your work environment. By creating a space that fosters this positive energy, your business model will attract clients who resonate with your mission and values. In turn, this cultivates a loyal customer base so it becomes a win/win.

Lastly, work-life balance techniques involving spiritual practices must be incorporated into a sustainable business plan. You should always prioritize personal development and self-care in addition to your work obligations if you want to achieve Soulful Success. You can prevent burnout and keep your enthusiasm for your work by setting boundaries and making time for introspection and renewal. A spiritual framework combined with visionary business planning guarantees that the journey will continue to be rewarding and that the company will continue to be a tool for both individual and group transformation. In the end, you can manifest abundance while staying true to your purpose and values by developing a sustainable business model.

CHAPTER 10

Cultivating a Supportive Community

The Importance of Connection in Business

The success of any business endeavor is largely dependent on connection, especially for those looking to incorporate spirituality into their business endeavors. Understanding the value of connection can change the way we approach our work in a society that frequently places more emphasis on rivalry than teamwork. For you, this relationship is more than just networking; it represents a profound, innate comprehension of a common goal and growth. You can create environments that not only support your personal goals but also improve your communities by cultivating sincere relationships.

Fundamentally, connection in business refers to establishing sincere bonds of respect, trust, and empathy. This entails establishing forums where candid communication and vulnerability are welcomed for spiritual entrepreneurs. Collaborations and partnerships are stronger when people feel heard and seen. In addition to fostering innovation and creativity, this strategy supports the spiritual idea of unity. When everyone contributes their special business talents, the combined energy can produce remarkable results and create a synergy that goes beyond conventional business dealings.

Mindfulness-based strategies play a pivotal role in fostering these connections. By incorporating practices such as active listening and mindful communication, business professionals can deepen their relationships with clients, colleagues, and stakeholders. This mindful approach encourages an atmosphere of presence and awareness, where each interaction becomes an opportunity for growth and learning. When you prioritize presence in your interactions, you not only enhance your own well-being but also create a ripple effect that positively influences all of your connections.

The energy we bring into our business dealings significantly affects the connections we form. Remember that with your energy healing techniques you can maintain a balanced and vibrant energy field, which is crucial for attracting like-minded individuals. By continuously aligning your personal energy with your business intentions, you will manifest connections that are not only beneficial but also deeply fulfilling. This alignment will also help in creating a work environment that resonates with abundance and purpose, ultimately leading to a more enriched business journey.

Incorporating meaningful connections into your business operations can lead to a deep sense of fulfillment and purpose. Realizing that business is a platform for spiritual expression rather than merely a means to an end can be incredibly freeing for people who are spiritually inclined. The sense of community and belonging grows stronger as connections do, turning the workplace into a sacred space for development and exploration. You can move through your business endeavors with clarity, purpose, and an unwavering dedication to uplifting others and yourself on the path to Soulful Success by embracing the significance of connection.

Building Networks with Like-Minded Individuals

Building networks with like-minded individuals is a transformative process that not only enhances your business journey but will also enrich your spiritual growth. As a spiritual seeker, you understand that surrounding yourself with individuals who share similar values and aspirations can significantly impact everything along your journey. This section will explore the importance of cultivating these networks and offers practical insights on how to connect with others who resonate with your vision of Soulful Success.

Determining your basic beliefs and goals is the first step in creating a network of people who share your values. Think about the facets of spirituality and business that most appeal to you, whether it's coaching, energy healing, or mindfulness. You can look for people who share your values once you have a clear idea of your own mission. This common ground will encourage closer ties and establish a nurturing atmosphere where cooperation and development can thrive. Keep in mind that the energy you expend when being true to yourself will draw people who share your vibration.

Meeting people who are passionate about spiritual business and entrepreneurship can be accomplished through attending workshops, retreats, and even online communities. These areas frequently offer chances for deep conversations and teamwork, enabling you to share experiences, share ideas, and encourage one another on your paths. Joining networks or professional organizations that emphasize spiritual business practices is another option. Making connections with people in these contexts can result in beneficial alliances and mentoring relationships that advance your knowledge of how to incorporate spirituality into your business journey and any professional activities.

Social media platforms can also serve as powerful tools for building your network. Engaging in discussions, sharing insights, and showcasing your work can attract like-minded individuals who resonate with your message. Platforms like Facebook groups, LinkedIn, and Instagram are excellent for finding communities centered around spiritual business professionals. By actively participating in these online spaces, you can cultivate relationships that may eventually evolve into collaborative projects or supportive friendships, all contributing to your overall sense of belonging in this vibrant community.

Nurturing these connections requires ongoing effort and genuine engagement. Take the time to reach out, share resources, and celebrate the successes of those within your network. Building a community is never just about what you can gain but also about what you can contribute. Offer your support, share your expertise, and practice active listening. As you invest in these relationships, you will find that they become a source of inspiration, encouragement, and accountability, propelling you toward your vision of Soulful Success. In this way, your network becomes not just a collection of contacts but a sacred community that uplifts and empowers each member on their unique journey.

Utilizing Group Energy for Collective Success

In the realm of spiritual business professionals, harnessing the collective energy of a group is a powerful catalyst for success. This concept transcends traditional business strategies, inviting us to explore the synergy that emerges when like-minded individuals unite with a shared purpose. Within this collective energy lies an abundance of creativity, motivation, and inspiration, all of which can be directed toward achieving common goals. By cultivating an environment that values collaboration and mutual support, you can create a transformative space where individual strengths are amplified, and the collective consciousness is elevated.

To effectively utilize group energy, it is essential to establish a clear vision that resonates with all members of the group. This vision acts as a guiding light, aligning everyone's intentions and efforts. When participants feel connected to a greater purpose, they are more likely to invest their energy wholeheartedly into the endeavor. Creating an inclusive atmosphere where each voice is heard will foster trust and commitment, enabling individuals to contribute their unique perspectives and talents. This alignment not only enhances creativity but also strengthens the bonds between group members, cultivating a sense of belonging that is critical for long- term success.

Mindfulness practices will also play a pivotal role in harnessing group energy. Participants can center themselves and tune into the collective vibration by utilizing techniques like energy healing sessions, breathwork, or group meditation. These exercises facilitate a deeper connection for the group in addition to clearing personal obstacles. When participants enter a state of mindfulness together, they can synchronize their energies, creating a powerful force that propels the group toward its goals. This energy sustains the idea that success is a shared journey rather than an individual endeavor. All group members are strengthened by this shared experience, which creates an atmosphere of acceptance and support.

Additionally, the effectiveness of group energy is increased when spiritual principles are incorporated into business strategies. A spiritual approach to problems fosters a mindset of abundance rather than scarcity, and promotes cooperation over rivalry. People in a group are more likely to help one another, share resources, and celebrate successes together when they believe that your success as a whole is interconnected. This change in viewpoint not only improves the group's performance as a whole but also fits with the core principles of Soulful Success, which gauges success by the positive effects one has on the community and the wider world.

To sum up, utilizing group energy is not merely about achieving business objectives; it is about creating a vibrant community that thrives on shared intentions and spiritual growth. When we embrace a culture of collaboration, mindfulness, and abundance, we can unlock the full potential of our collective efforts. This approach not only enhances personal fulfillment but also contributes to the greater good, ensuring that success is not just a personal achievement but a collective victory. You will be able to handle your business journey with poise, purpose, and a deep sense of interconnectedness if you adopt this philosophy of Soulful Success.

CHAPTER 11

The Journey Ahead: Sustaining Soulful Success

Continuous Growth and Learning

Continuous growth and learning are fundamental components of a soulful approach to success. In the journey of spiritual seekers, especially those engaged in business ventures, the pursuit of knowledge and self- improvement is not merely a pathway to professional advancement but a holistic practice that deepens one's connection to purpose and fulfillment. By embracing continuous growth, you can align your business strategies with your spiritual values, fostering not just external success but also internal harmony. This alignment serves as a powerful catalyst for creating meaningful impact in both personal and professional realms.

At the heart of continuous growth is the commitment to lifelong learning. Spiritual seekers often discover that each experience, whether a success or a setback, is a valuable lesson that contributes to your overall journey.

In the context of business, this can manifest as a willingness to adapt and innovate. Mindfulness-based business strategies encourage professionals to stay present and aware, allowing them to respond to challenges with clarity and creativity. By cultivating a mindset of curiosity and openness, you can transform obstacles into opportunities for growth, enhancing your resilience and ability to thrive in a dynamic business landscape.

Your learning process can also be greatly improved by incorporating spiritual practices into your everyday routine. For instance, you can overcome emotional obstacles and limiting beliefs that prevent you from growing by using energy healing techniques. You can also make room for introspection and insight by practicing techniques like breathwork, visualization, or meditation. In addition to aiding in your personal growth, this inward work affects how you relate to clients, coworkers, and the larger community. As a result, a deeper comprehension of your purpose and the global impact of your work becomes entwined with the learning process.

By assisting you in discovering your own strengths and passions, spiritual life and business coaching is essential for promoting ongoing development. Setting goals that align with your true self is made possible by coaches who incorporate spiritual wisdom into their coaching sessions. This method goes beyond traditional measures of accomplishment and promotes a deeper investigation of what success actually means on a soul level. A more balanced and satisfying work life can result from this reflective process, which frequently reveals new opportunities for development that are consistent with your values.

Spiritually based visionary business planning will inspire you to think clearly and purposefully about your future. In order to create a roadmap that reflects both material success and spiritual growth, this forward-thinking approach highlights the significance of coordinating business goals with spiritual aspirations. You can foster an atmosphere of creativity and abundance by consistently honing this vision via education and self-improvement. In the end, the process of constant learning and development not only benefits you personally but also helps bring about a societal awakening that motivates others to strive for their own Soulful Success.

Embracing Change and Transformation

Since change is the only thing that is constant, accepting change and transformation is a crucial part of any spiritual journey, especially when you are pursuing entrepreneurship. As spiritual seekers, we frequently find ourselves juggling the inherent uncertainties that come with major life transitions while at the intersection of our professional and personal development. It's critical to realize that change is an opportunity for significant growth rather than just a disruption. It encourages you to develop resilience and adaptability, two critical traits that help us deal with the challenges of both our inner and outer lives.

Change also will always serves as a catalyst for deeper self- awareness and will benefit collective consciousness. When you embrace transformation, you align your business practices with your core values, allowing authenticity to guide your decisions. This alignment fosters a sense of purpose that resonates not only within ourselves but also with our clients, colleagues and communities. By integrating your mindfulness- based strategies, you will cultivate a state of presence that helps you respond to change with clarity and intention, rather than reacting impulsively out of fear or resistance.

Soul-centered entrepreneurship thrives on the premise that our businesses can be reflections of our spiritual journeys. By welcoming change, you open yourself to innovative ideas and fresh perspectives that can elevate your ventures. This process may involve redefining your goals, re-evaluating your offerings, or even shifting your target audience. Each transformation, no matter how daunting, can lead to greater alignment with your soul's mission, ultimately enhancing your ability to serve others. As we learn to view challenges as stepping stones rather than obstacles, we empower ourselves to create impactful solutions that resonate with the world around us.

As you encounter shifts in your business landscape, remember how crucial it is to maintain your energetic balance. Energy healing can play a vital role in supporting you through periods of transformation. Your daily practices such as meditation, breathwork, and energy clearing can help you release limiting beliefs and emotional blockages that may hinder your allowing necessary change. Incorporating these healing modalities into your routines, you can create a stable foundation from which to embrace change. This energetic alignment will enhance your personal well- being and also radiates into your professional environments, fostering a culture of positivity and innovation.

Embracing change and transformation is a journey that is closely connected to the concepts of bringing things into existence and having abundance in life. Acknowledging that each change brings forth opportunities enables you to develop a mindset grounded in gratitude and openness. This outlook empowers you to draw towards your opportunities that resonate with your highest potential.

As we navigate the highs and lows in business, we must remember that transformation is not just about seeing external success; it's also about nurturing our inner selves. We must remember to utilize our spiritual practices to establish a positive work-life balance so we can create successful companies and happy, purposeful lives.

Celebrating Your Soulful Achievements

Integrating spiritual wisdom into your business journey requires you to celebrate your soulful accomplishments with good reason. Since Soulful Success encompasses more than just material gain and also involves personal development, a metamorphosis takes place during the journey. Acknowledging and celebrating these accomplishments when they happen helps you become more in tune with your soul's calling and strengthens your bond with your purpose. Let's discuss the value of acknowledging your accomplishments, no matter how small, and how doing so can greatly improve your overall business journey.

When we think of achievements, it is easy to focus solely on tangible results like revenue milestones or client acquisitions. On the other hand, soulful accomplishments frequently show up as breakthroughs in your own life, such as improved intuition, or a renewed sense of purpose in your endeavors. These epiphanies may involve conquering a fear, learning a new skill, or improving your comprehension of the needs of your clients. By recognizing these turning points, you develop a comprehensive picture of your path and strengthen the notion that every action, no matter how minor, advances your ultimate goal.

Including celebration in your daily routine can also be a very effective way to practice mindfulness. By stopping to consider all of your achievements, you develop an awareness of the here and now and the progress you have made. In addition to relieving the pressure to always aim higher, this practice will help promote appreciation for every accomplishment. Celebrating your soulful accomplishments, whether through journaling, meditation, or even simple rituals, can develop into a sacred practice that helps you stay grounded in your purpose and improves your general wellbeing.

For individuals involved in soul-centered entrepreneurship activities, it's crucial to acknowledge and celebrate their successes for community reasons. It highlights the belief that business isn't just about achieving external goals but also about finding inner satisfaction. This approach changes the emphasis from being competitive and making comparisons to fostering collaboration and a sense of community. It helps in creating an environment where spiritual entrepreneurs can flourish together. Sharing any of your achievements with those who share mindsets not only enhances your happiness but also motivates others on their paths. This leads to a chain reaction of positivity and support, within your circle of connections.

Celebrating your achievements means recognizing the unique path you're on and valuing the enthusiasm you put into your work. This reaffirms your commitment to living a life driven by spirit and purpose and encourages you to embrace your growth. By incorporating this strategy into your daily routine, you'll find that it enhances your business success and spiritual development, enabling you to draw prosperity and contentment into every area of your life. Cherish the happy and successful times no matter how big or small. Allow them to guide you in the direction of success and development.

In closing, please remember our life and business experiences are always about the journey.

My passion is to help spiritual seekers find that balance and harmony between their spiritual path and business journey. We all came here to experience peace, love, joy, and abundance so if you're not having that experience, let's connect! *Sharon Hess*

ABOUT ME

I'm a Spiritual Business and Life Coach, Certified Reiki Master and Natural Healer, Akashic Record and Soul Story Master, Angel Artist, Amazon #1 New Release and International Best-Selling Author of "Spiritual Spice"

You can find me at www.SharonHess.com
www.Facebook.com/sharonkhess
www.LinkedIn.com/sharonhess
www.Instagram.com/sharonhesshealing
Email: Sharon@SharonHess.com

My website-